THIRTY CLOUDS

GEORGE SZIRTES
CLARISSA UPCHURCH

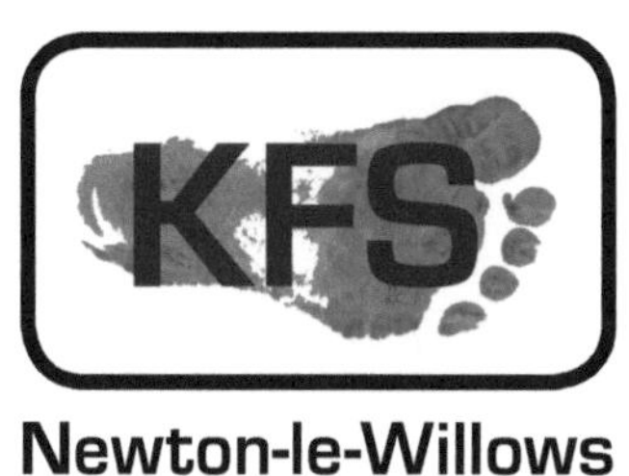

Newton-le-Willows

Published in the United Kingdom in 2019
by The Knives Forks And Spoons Press,
51 Pipit Avenue,
Newton-le-Willows,
Merseyside,
WA12 9RG.

ISBN 978-1-912211-29-6

Acknowledgements:

All texts and images were exhibited at Thirty Clouds (Wymondham Arts, Centre 2017), and a selection in a travelling exhibition, transARTations: wandering texts, travelling objects (2017). 'Cloud 19 (was 3)' was exhibited in the Blackpool Illuminations in 2018.

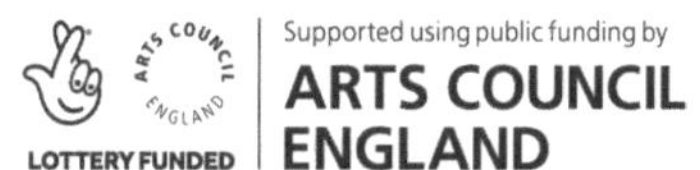

THIRTY CLOUDS

Note on Thirty Clouds

This book is a collaboration between visual artist Clarissa Upchurch and poet George Szirtes. Upchurch's images came first and the text followed based on free interpretations in the form of cinquains combined with prose poems.

The thirty visual works here are all based on ***monoprints***, a process whereby ink is printed directly from freshly painted metal surface, so each printed image is unique. It offers painterly effects hard to achieve by other printing methods.

The ***cinquain*** is a poetic form invented by the American poet Adelaide Crapsey (1878-1914). It consists of five lines that break down into a syllabic pattern of 2-4-6-8-2. The effect can be that of the breath expanding for the first four lines then being let out in the fifth.

Cloud 1

Rising
from the water
clouds emerge as light,
blinding, elemental, stiff, stuck,
too much.

Waking was a kind of flower that billowed through the window, its petals distraught. I was a very small child. My mother lay beside me. Those were her eyes, or the whites of her eyes, or the whiteness of her cheeks or breasts. I woke to this, as from the sea, rising.

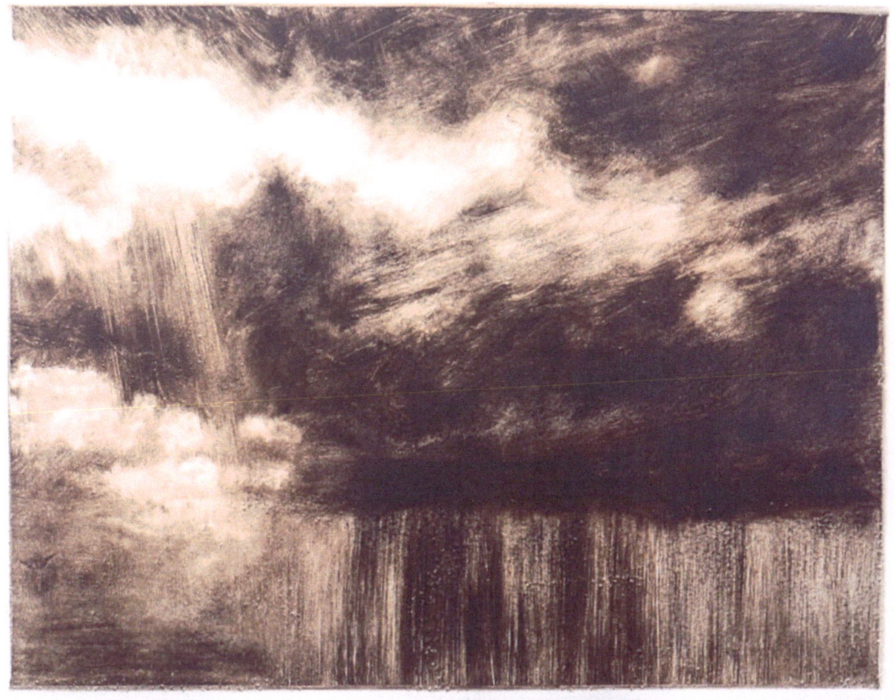

Cloud 2

Moments
of rain falling
in contrary patterns.
The darkness is concentrated
then spread.

There were moments of sheer fury. I had grown used to seeing her angry, to feeling the force of her anger without understanding it but feeling, inside me, a responding thunder that demanded its own life. Outside lay the street I couldn't yet see or know. Outside, the furies gathered into language, thunder with moments of rain.

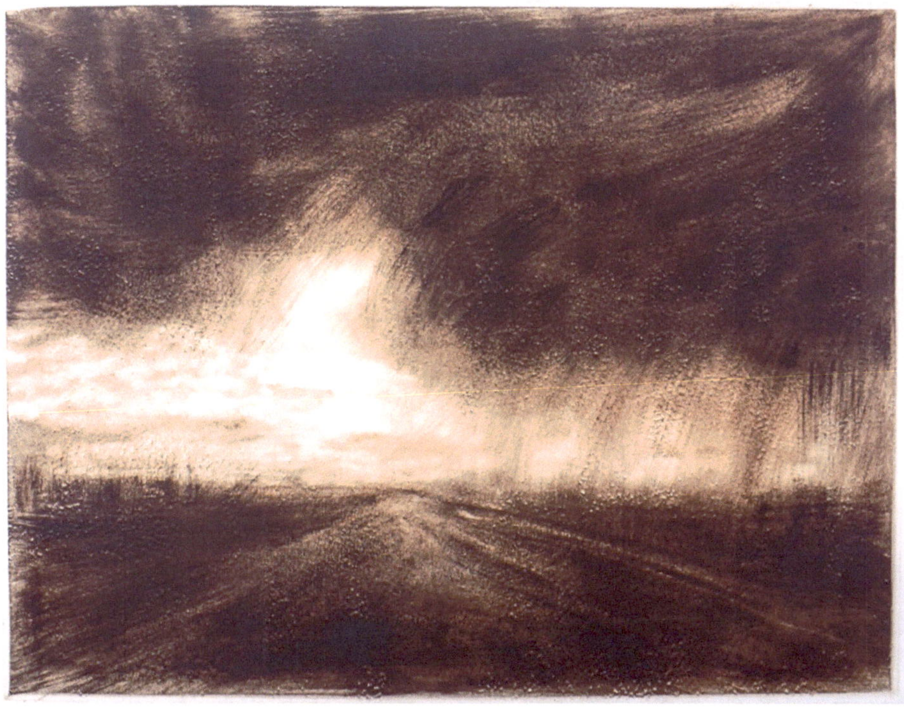

Cloud 3

The war
in the sky is
the war in the eye. Dreams
destroy each other. We become
our dreams.

We were watching the film when the cinema exploded. The sky was shot full of holes. It was only a game and we were only children, but this was real. What we imagined had come to life. What we imagined was there in the sky. It was staring us in the face. We put on our pyjamas and waited.

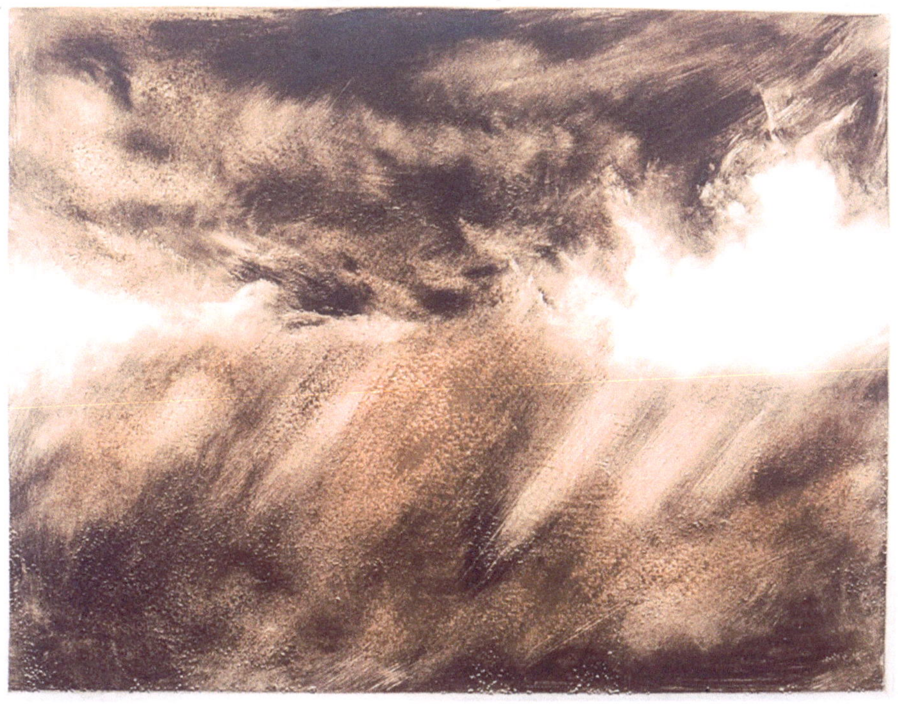

Cloud 4

You toss
your hair. It burns.
It is as though figures
of speech could catch fire and consume
the head.

People run across burning coals, their feet undamaged, the conflagration inside them. When she tossed her hair the room was black fire. Her eyes were bigger than usual. You see things and assimilate them into incomprehensible patterns like this. Nonetheless, they are patterns: a flung head, a blaze of cloud, your hair on fire.

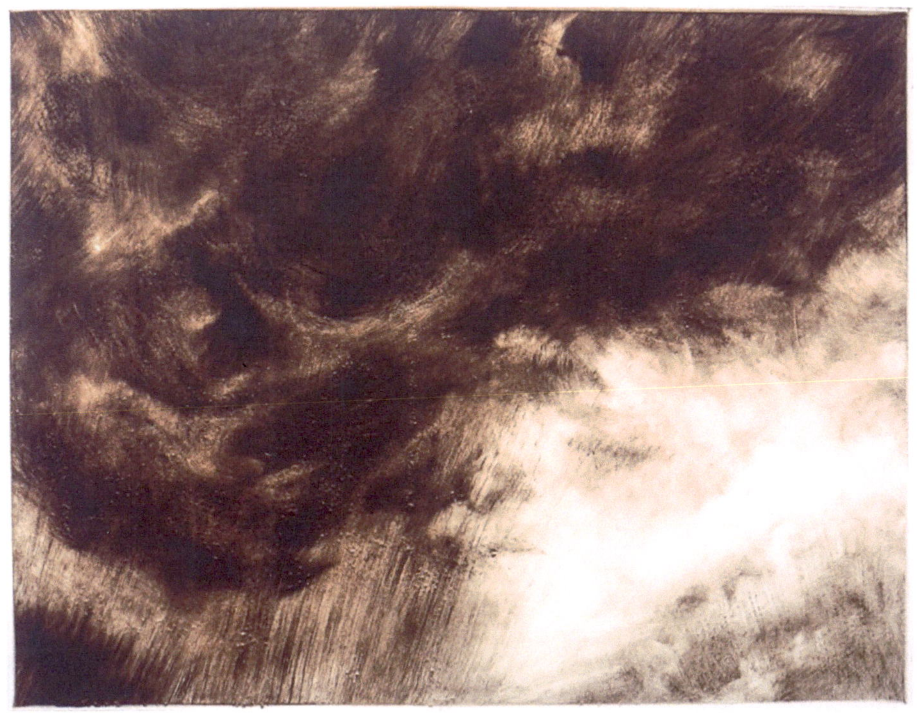

Cloud 5

Clouds part.
The sea's on fire!
Newton, Democritus,
gather skirts to dance on Blake's shores
of light.

The mystical experience is inevitably of light. They saw a bright light before them. They entered the fields / shores of light. The light of the world was alight. The fire in their hearts was on fire. Their tongues were burning. Then some burned out. Others burned up and are still burning on the horizon. They have been transformed. They are dust. They have gone. They have seen the light.

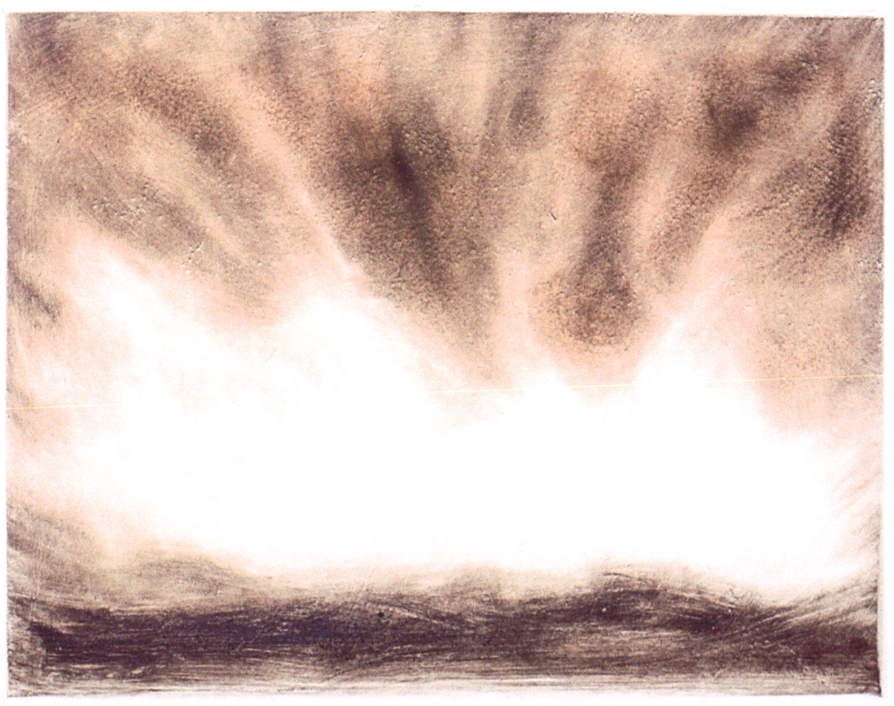

Cloud 6

Back then
clouds were hands, dark,
scooping up what remained
of sky as if to shield us from
ourselves.

The hand of god in Africa is African. To the white child in his snowbound city it is no more real than his image in the mirror which is elsewhere, beyond the mirror, at a vast remove and still travelling, further and further off, the distance constantly growing until all the air in the room has been sucked out and he is gasping for air. Africa! he cries. Bring me air! Bring me Africa!

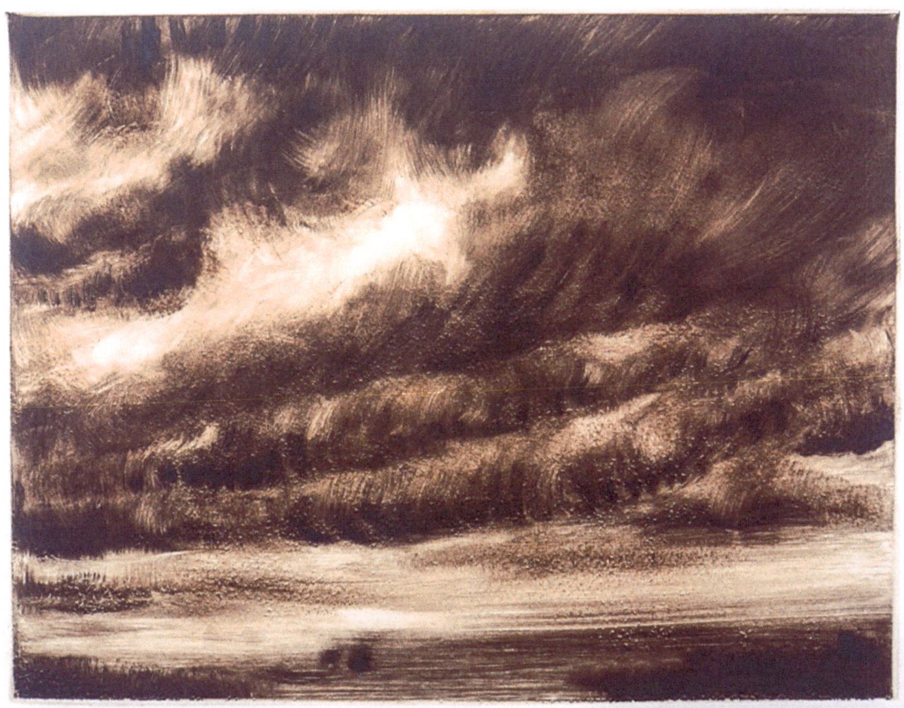

Cloud 7

As if
clouds could speak. Light
launches itself into
image. Here comes the ocean, dense
with foam.

Something consumes you. Something is eating you away like the sea at the foot of a cliff but it's only an undefined turbulence. Clouds present themselves as evidence, so you open the file and read. The reading itself is consuming. Ocean becomes text, oceanic writing at the foot of a cliff that is half eaten away, like any text or any cloud.

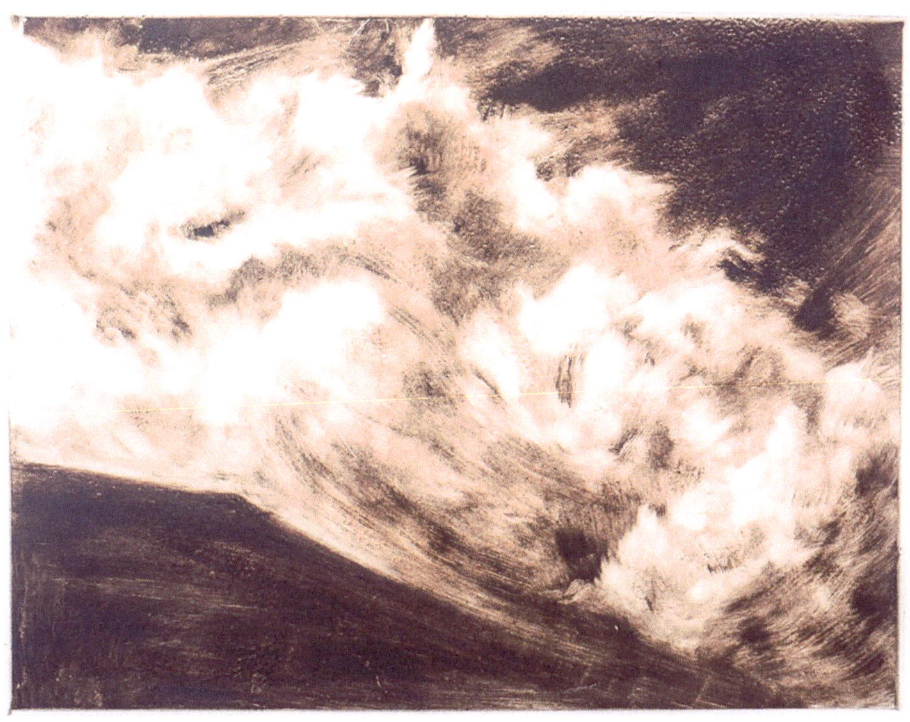

Cloud 8

Sometimes
a conference
of ghosts. Sometimes the gods
at home. Fierce talking heads. The rain
mid-speech.

As a child at the feet of adults. As a baby crawling under the table naked. As a figure in a crib. As a mouth. As urine. As fish. As perception. As heartbeat. There were giants everywhere in those days. There were gods in trousers. In conference glowering among the distant mountains. There were tribunals, judges, the soft authority of the breast.

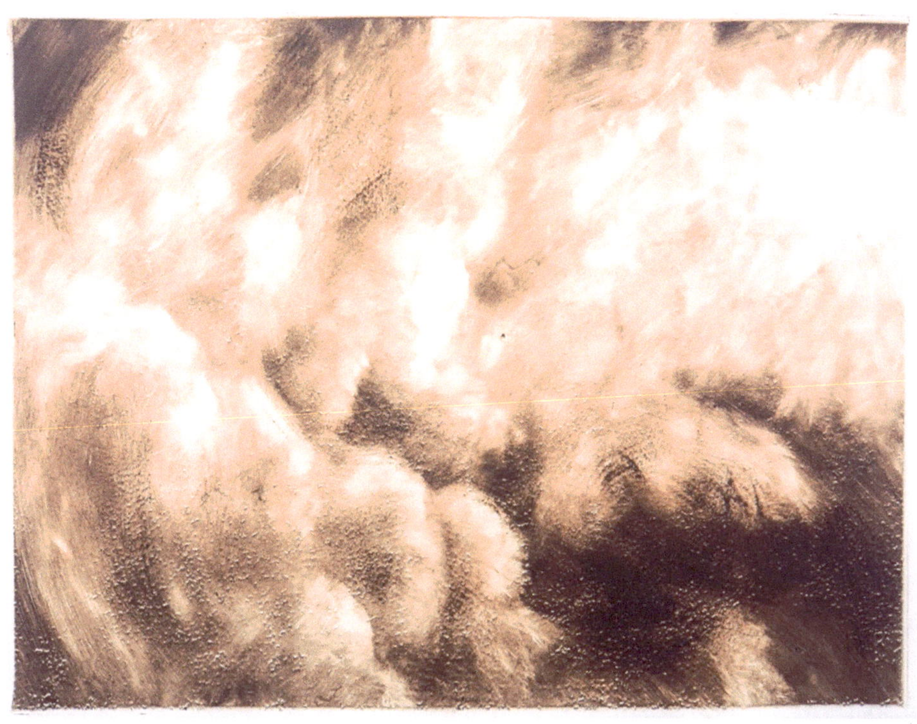

Cloud 9

The herd
is stampeding
to thunderous applause.
We are the Valkyrie! They yell
their names.

It was when the crowd pushed forward and everyone stumbled that the danger became apparent. They pushed and began to run. But we applauded them in their wildness and spectacle. We always do, even when running, even when falling, even when dying. Death is when the danger becomes apparent. More, we demanded. Give us death! Give us more of it!

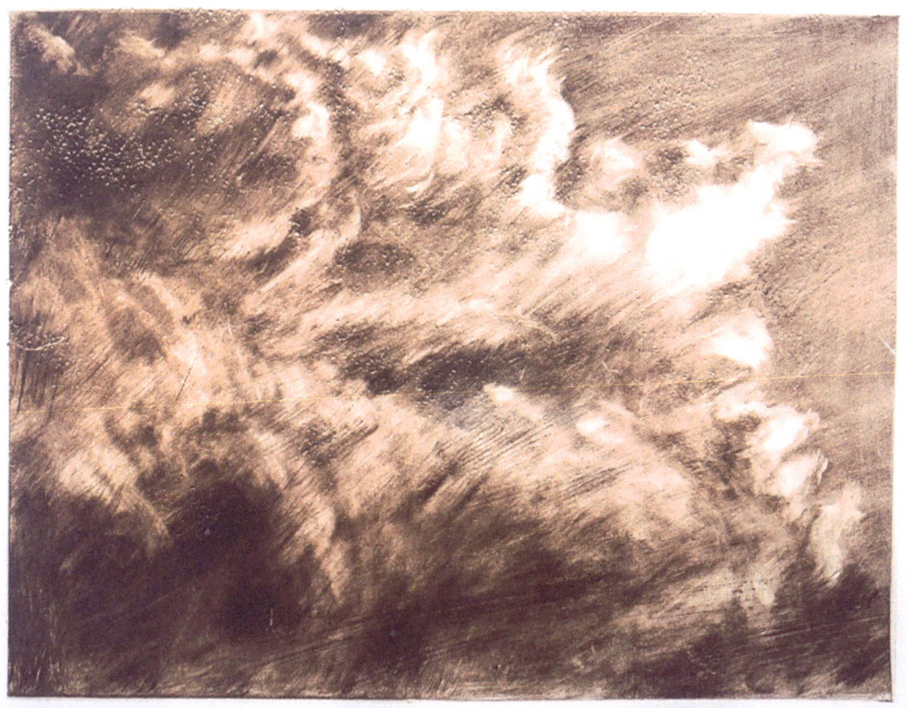

Cloud 10

A whisk
of tail. A pale
stink in the yard. Small flames.
Cloud language. Interpretation
of tongue.

We are objects of pity. Our brilliant tails are the best of us. Our eyes are melancholy, our mouths turned down. All we have is the sky with its airy nothings. When we ride it we feel a vague consolation. We are clouds left to regard ourselves, to interpret ourselves. It's a hard job. Believe me, it stinks.

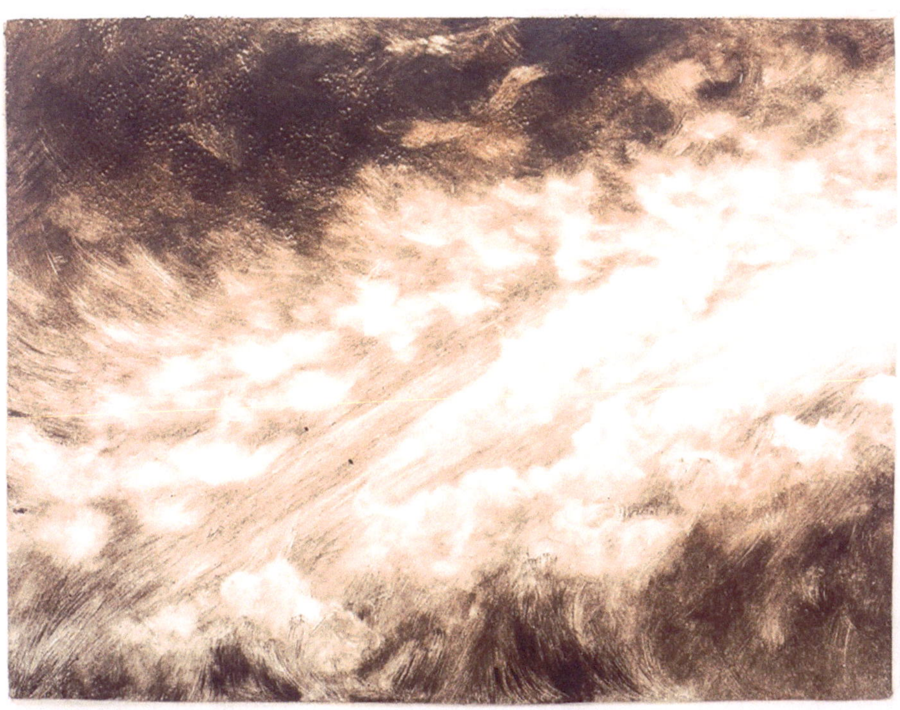

Cloud 11

Then it
was a blazing
bouquet, haunted flowers
in flight from earth, like blown hair, flown
and burned.

The paraffin heater in the corner of the room hissed and roared then settled into a blue ring, still fierce but small and governeable. We were cousins, it and I, my own blue flame, low and well-behaved. They could come in and turn us down or blow us right out. We were kings of light in our warm nook. We were powers, plagues ready to be loosed upon the world.

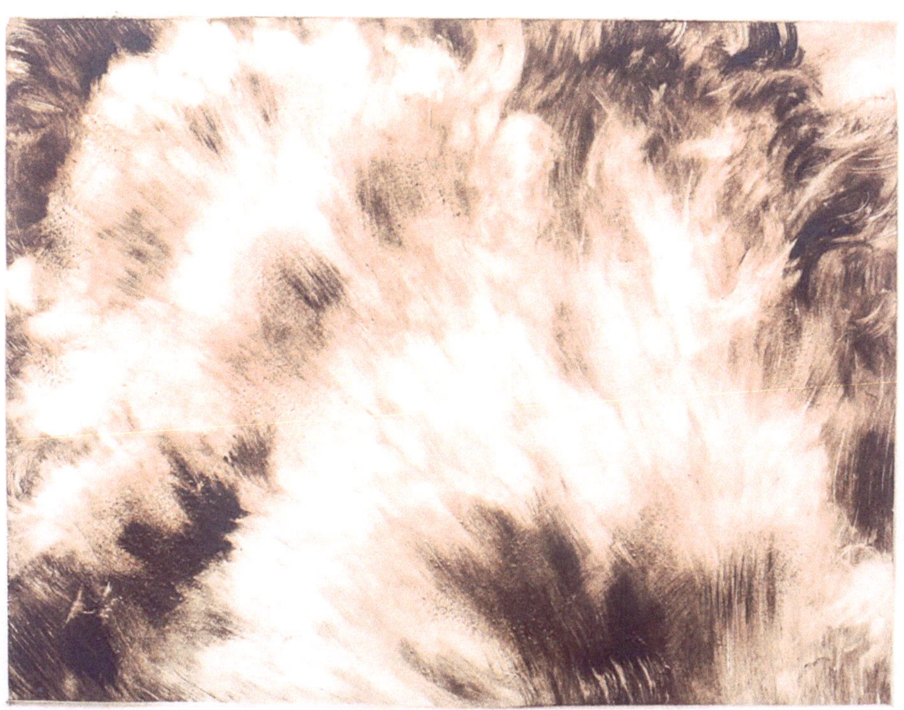

Cloud 12

They leaned
forward hoping
to observe the action.
Down below them the earth, sodden
with rain.

Welcome to the music hall, yes, you in your fancy boxes, you in your impeccable shirts, observers of spectacle, disappointing angels. Prepare to be entertained. Prepare for the miraculous intervention. Listen out and keep watching. Something unforgettable is about to happen. It is up to you to remember it.

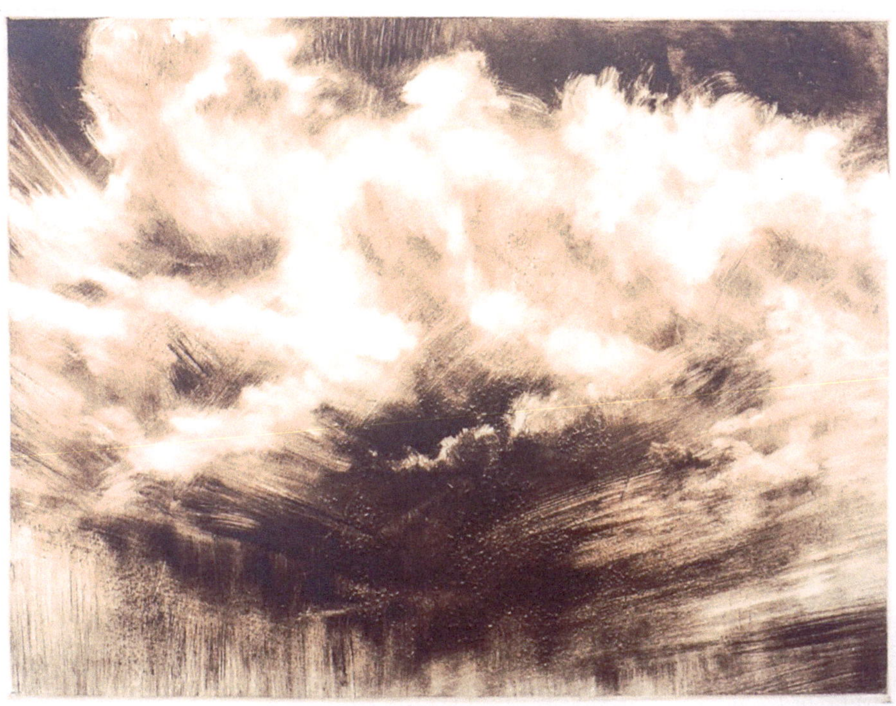

Cloud 13

Here is
the snakepit of
our half-finished business.
We must keep our creatures on a
tight leash!

Before the world began, in the belly of the universe, chaos gave birth to a forerunner. It was like this world, violent, incapable of acting in concert. We ate each other up. We tore each other to pieces. Then the universe stuck us back together and told us to get on with it. Be your own mothers and fathers, it said. Grow your own teeth. Tame your own mad hearts.

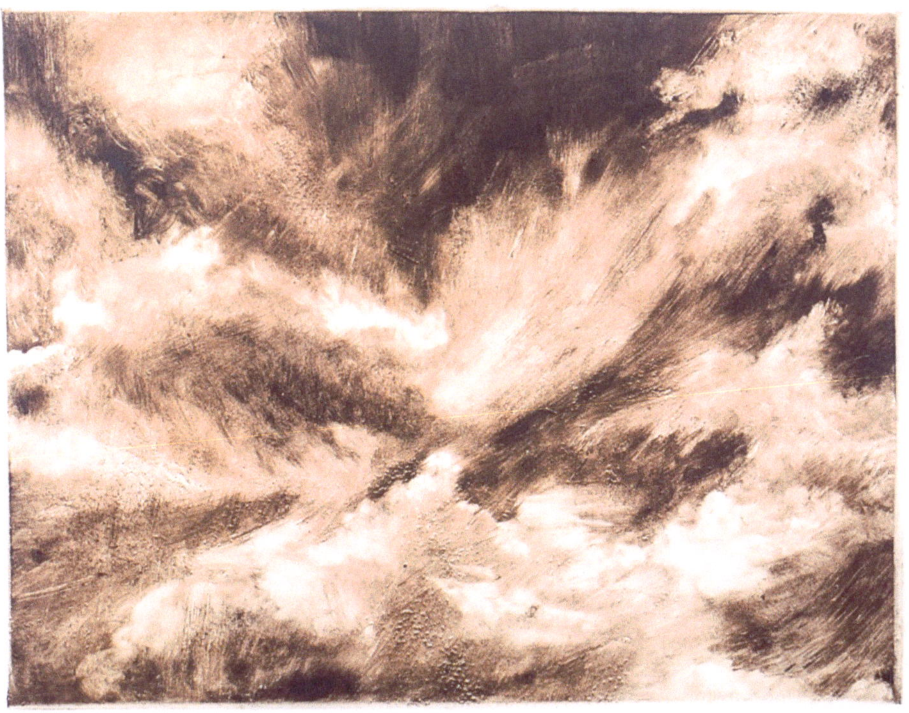

Cloud 14

Tiny
creatures will be
consumed by those larger
than themselves. So say the fleas, so
the whales.

First day of school. The wolves were bigger than we thought, the bears larger still and, above all, the prehistoric monsters we had still to meet. On the school dome the large hirsute figure of King Kong beating his chest, and snatching at aeroplanes, deeply in love with all the lithe girls watching from windows. Almost pathetic. Almost vulnerable.

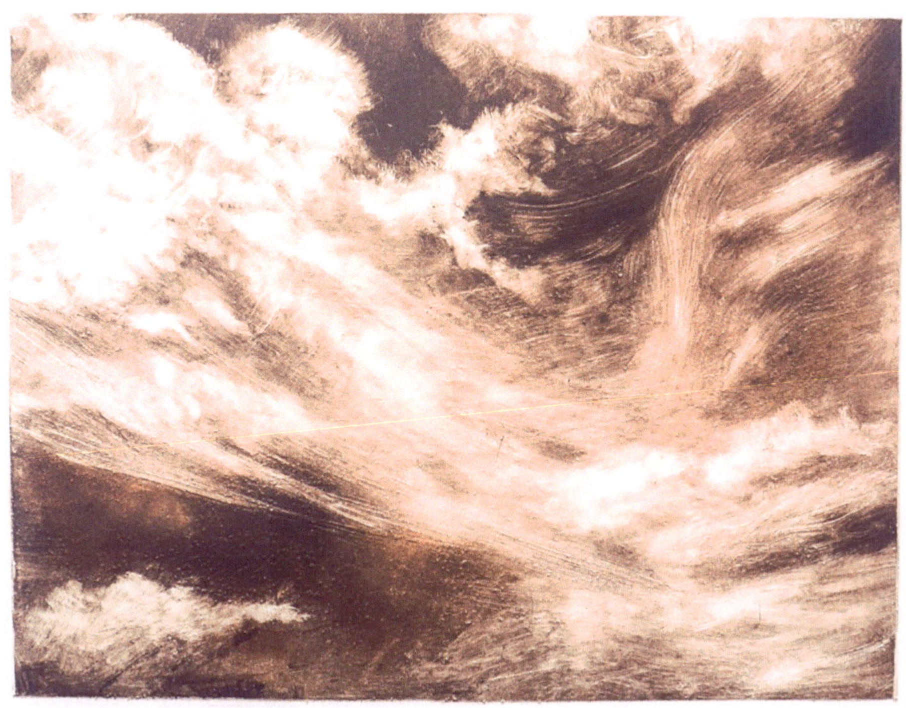

Cloud 15

The tide
swept us away.
One whoosh of sea and we
were gone only to resurface
dripping.

The tide bore them away to the Treacherous Isles. They were galley-slaves, pirates, wherrymen, sea-drenched. They foundered. They scrambled to shore. They crawled up the beach where they perished, their bones picked clean by albatrosses dressed as vultures. At least these were the stories they told each other afterwards, their bones still clean.

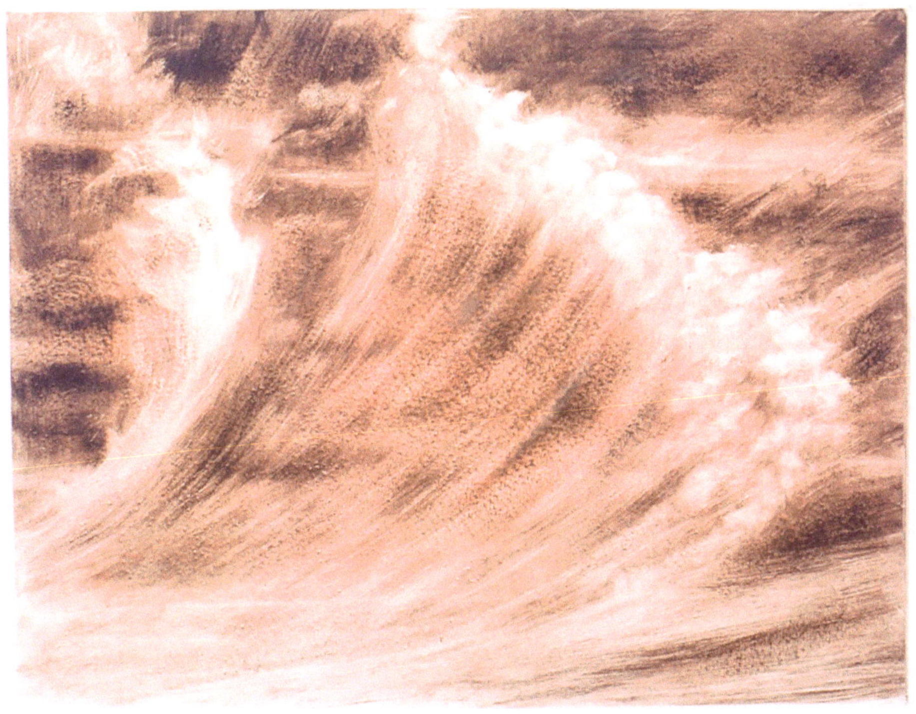

Cloud 16

And then
they spread their wings
and took pity. Angels
of mercy breathing over us
like glass.

After the mother, the father. After the father the grandmother. After the grandmother the grandfather. And so it proceeds. Ancestors in the wardrobe. Ancestors in the cellar. Ancestors in the fridge. Ancestors in the underground clogging the escalators in overcrowded stations full of empty trains carrying nothing but clouds.

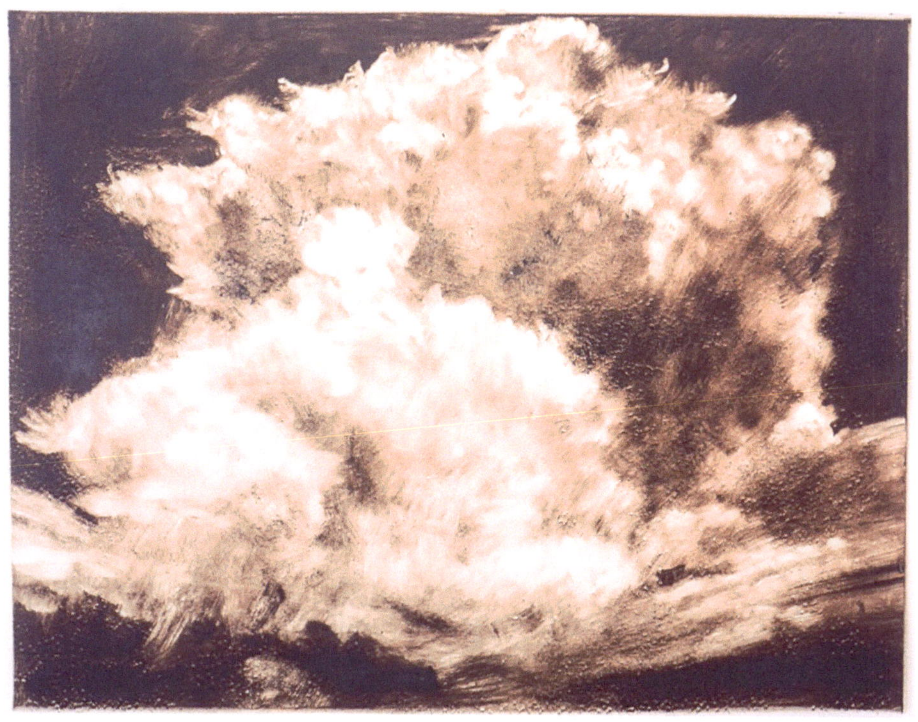

Cloud 17

The mouth
opens. It lives
alone. It breathes and gapes
like Odilon Redon but says
nothing.

The earliest dreams were forbidden. After that the ban was lifted but there came new dreams that had to be forbidden. Whatever was forbidden turned to dream. Then the dreams began to forbid themselves. But maybe they only dreamt they were forbidden. Meanwhile the bans produced more bans. This too is ban. This too is dream.

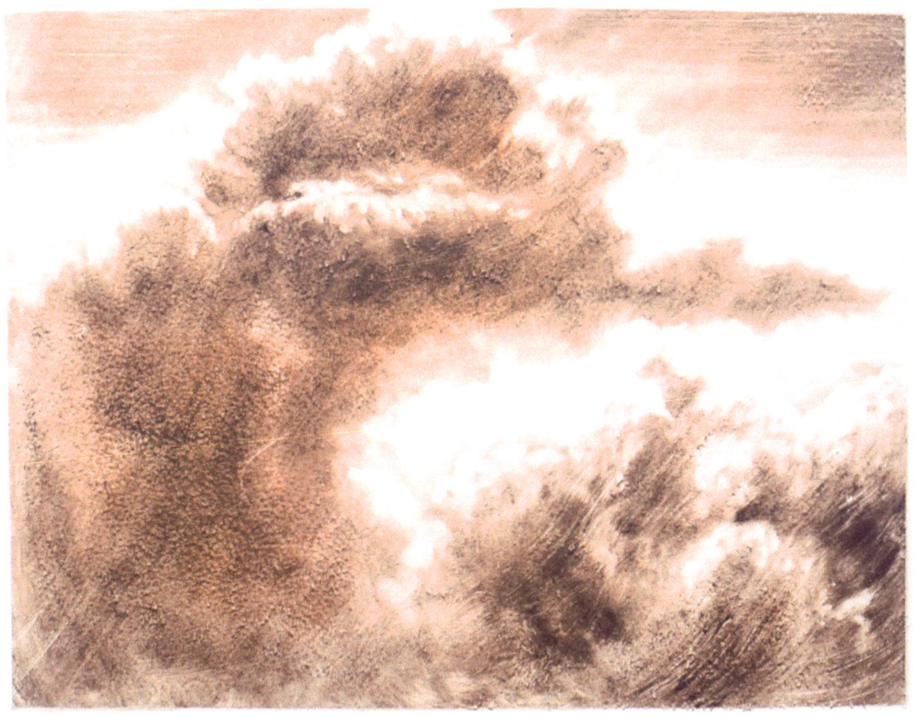

Cloud 18

The dead
lay on the ground,
whole families of them.
As above so below. As clouds
so men.

The first corpse I saw was covered in white dust. It lay in the street as if under a thin sprinkling of snow but it wasn't snowing. Later it did snow. Later the corpse was taken away and all that remained was the white dust in our heads which looked like snow but never melted. Then it did snow. Then there were more corpses.

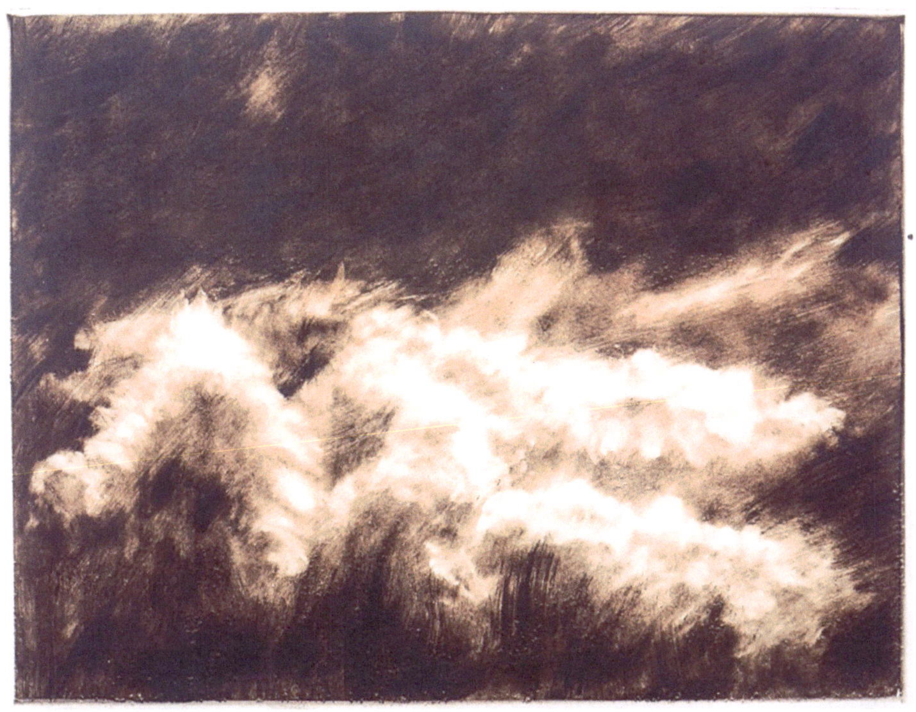

Cloud 19

The cloud
lay on its side
like a seal turning round
to face us, as if nature had
a face.

One learns as if in the cradle. It is as if night descended with the curtains. As if figures materialised in a doorway. Then they do materialise. Then night descends. Then clouds present us with faces as if that is what they had intended to do, as if clouds were whales, or castles, or promises, or threats, or selves, or a seal lying on the sand.

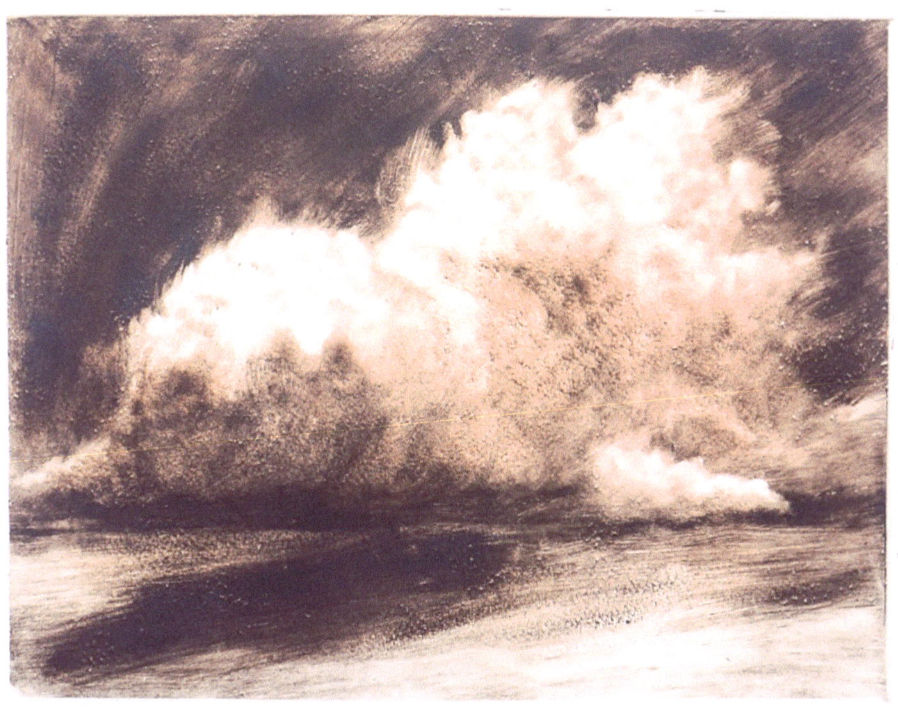

Cloud 20

I am
heavy. My heart
weighs a ton. It flowers
into density. Why? I have
no heart.

She was making bread, rolling dough, her shoulders pumping. It was as if she were moulding herself into a consumable, as if she were becoming dough, as if that were an ideal one might attain if only one had the stamina, the flour, the water, the salt, the sheer need. Here, she said. This is the oven. Let's wait to see what will happen.

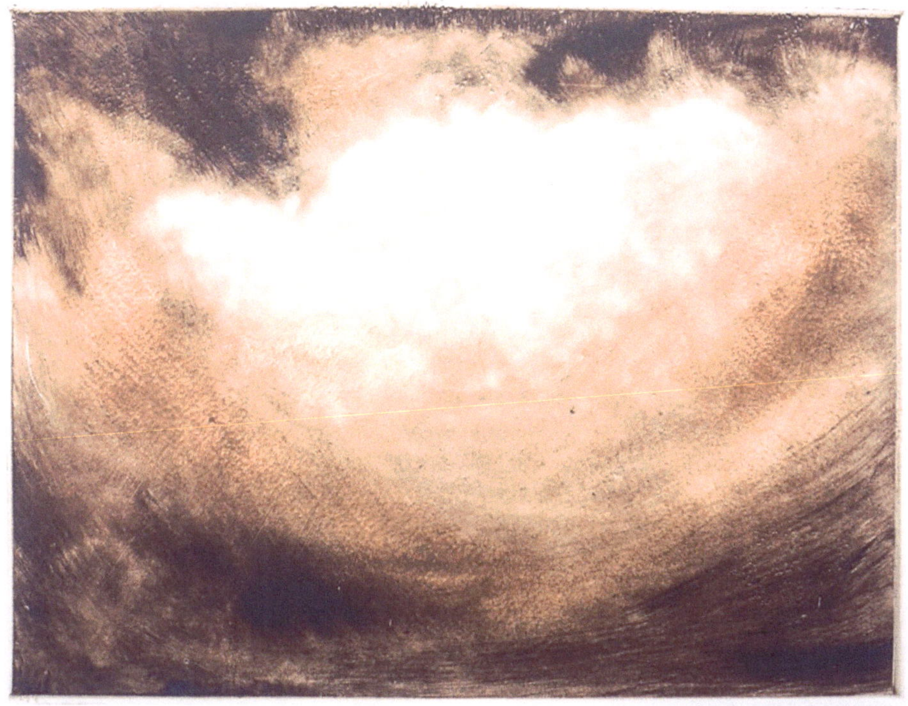

Cloud 21

Someone
left behind a
feather, so delicate
it could be blown away by light
alone.

She picked the feather from the ground. It was hardly more than fluff. But it was also a swan in a story she had once imagined, or imagined that she had imagined. One could only imagine so much, the rest was reality, wherever that lay, wherever it had been blown, wherever you could imagine it to have been blown.

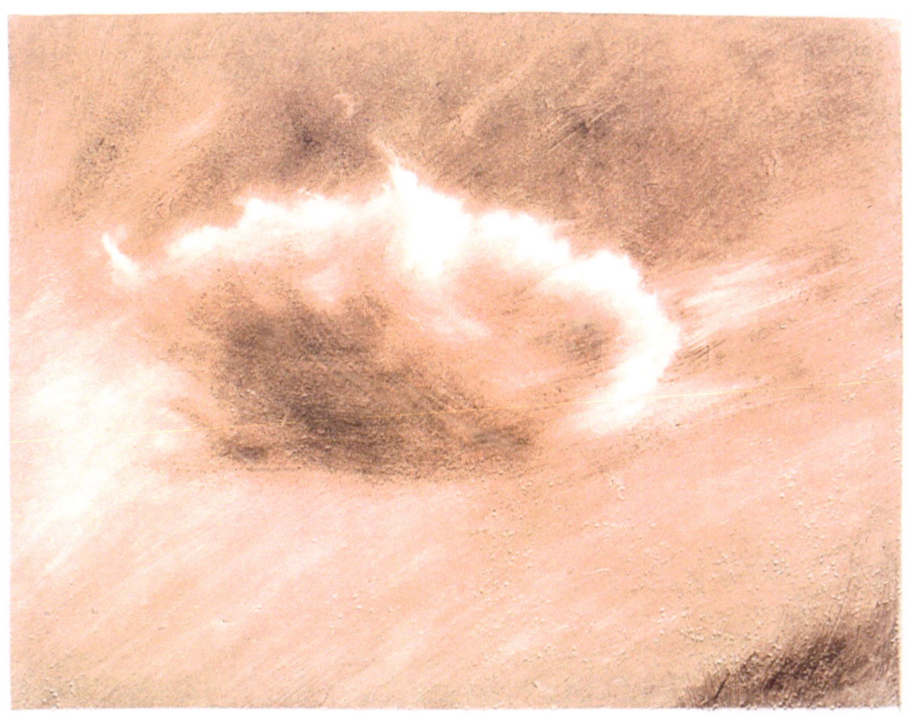

Cloud 22

After
the nebula
a spider, after that
a flower bursting from its own
dead light.

The elderly were sleeping in their chairs. The window was flickering with autumn. The house was empty. They were the house. These were their windows, lightly closed. Outside branches moved and leaves trembled. Outside birds were pecking on the lawn. They were in the house but the house was empty. They were waiting for the windows to open. They were waiting for their eyes.

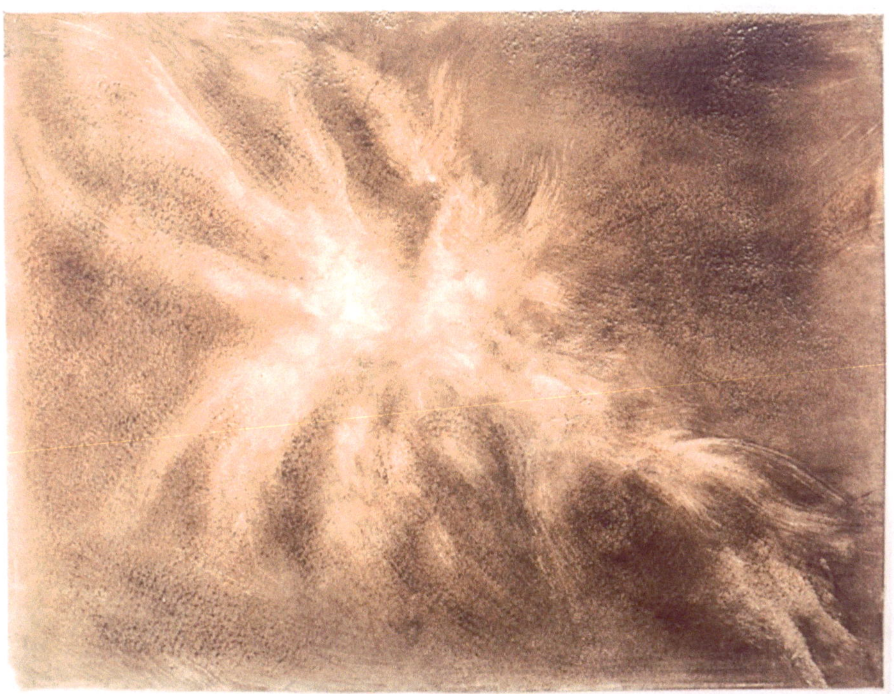

Cloud 23

You are
alone, small thing.
Do you find the sky vast?
Do you want us to pity you,
small thing?

Someone should have been waiting at the station. But there were other stations. They might have been waiting at one of them. So began the story they told each other while waiting. They had to invent the story. At each turn of the narrative they looked up to see if things had changed but they hadn't so they invented again. They took out a comma. Then they put it back in.

Cloud 24

Sometimes
an army rides
across a field. The field
registers it as downpour, as
ghost rain.

Limelight. The chorus line kicks. Underside of calf and thigh. A glitter at the crotch. Outside a train shudders past a field of corn. Outside someone lights a bonfire. Outside a man stubs out a cigarette. The chorus kicks again, advances a step then retreats. Outside the promise of rain advances and retreats. But this is inside.

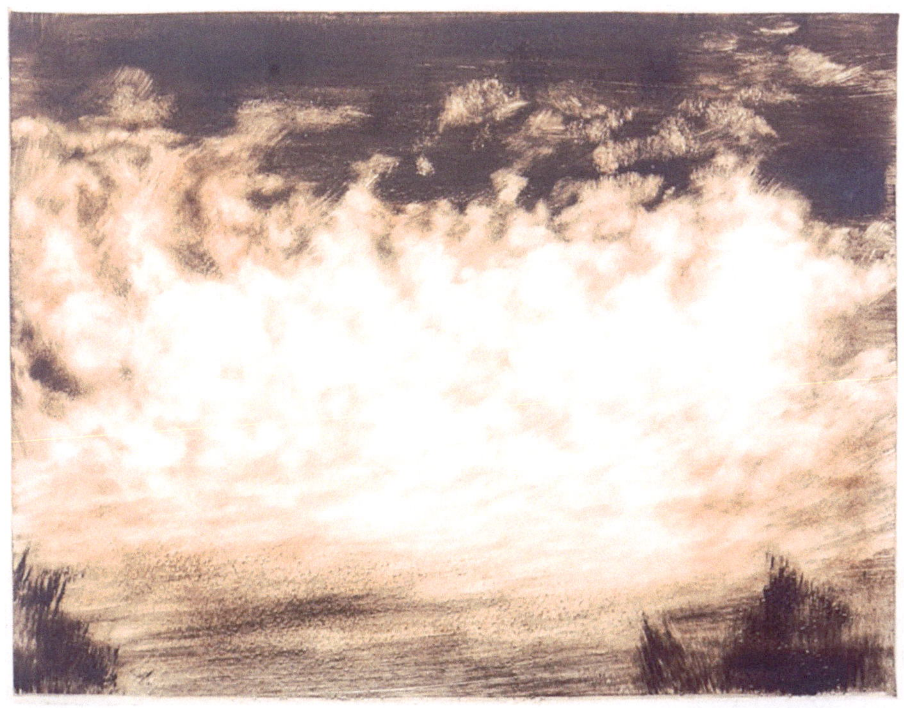

Cloud 25

Figures
at a window
pressing against the glass.
Bears perhaps, soft toys, heavier
than breath.

Back into childhood, through its discomforts, in through the front door and through to the room where you last saw yourself. Are you still there? Do you remember me? Are these your toys? Are these your wild shores? Is this your language? Is this the right house?

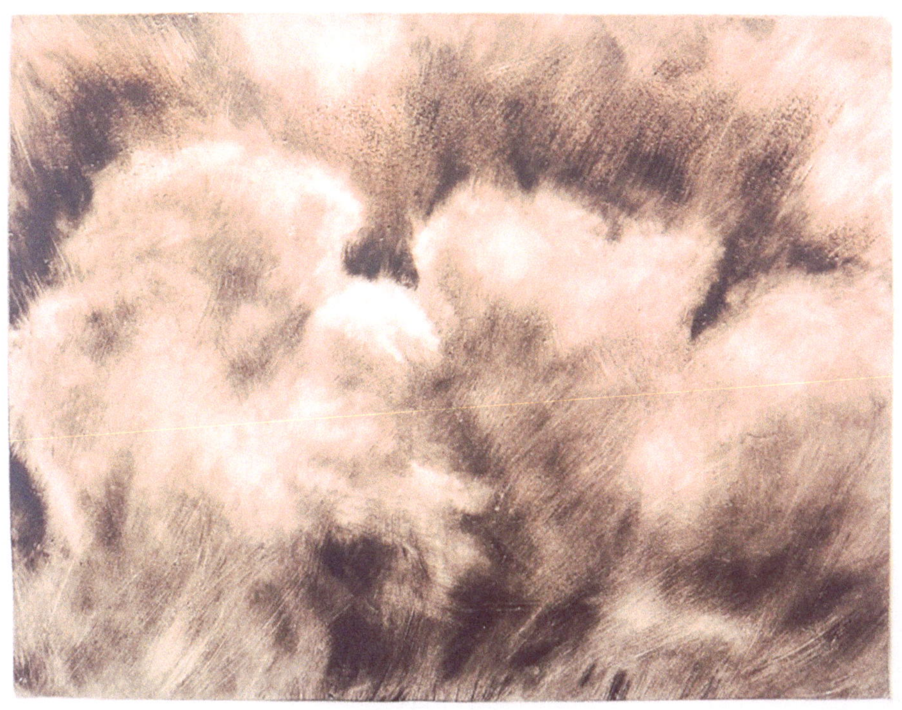

Cloud 26

Are those
alligators
or crocodiles gliding
through ambivalent waters filled
with stars?

Above us the archaic architecture of the sky. Would it hold up? Are its members secure? We wouldn't want it to come crashing down with all its monsters, with its metamorphic zoo and ominous weight. It is, after all, our attic. It is where we store things. Who knows how long it has been there? Who knows who built this crazy ramshackle mansion? If we had to start all over again we wouldn't start here.

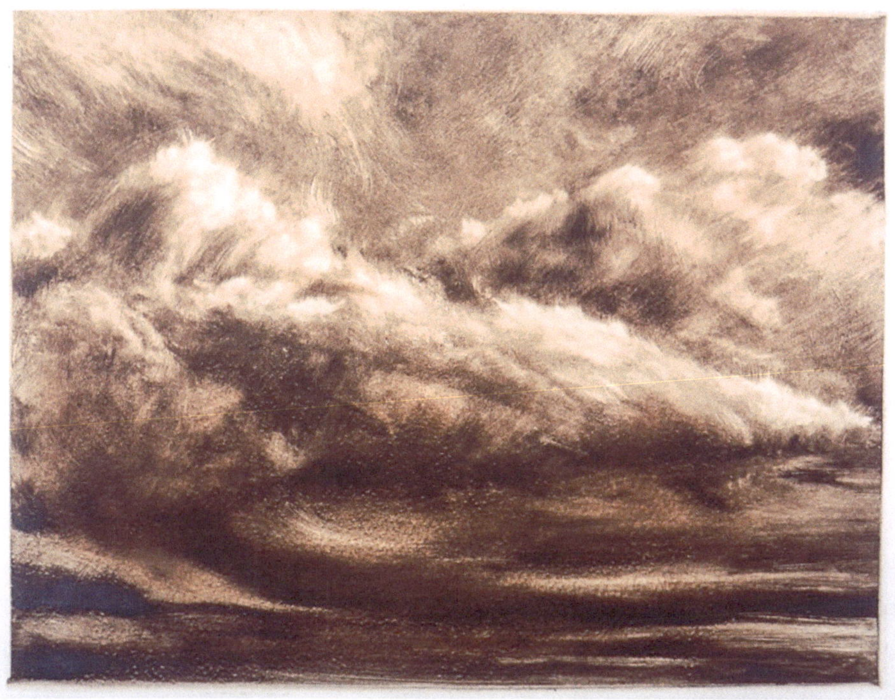

Cloud 27

Nothing
as regular
as regularity.
Clouds evenly spaced. Orderly
heavens.

We impose order on order and call it order, he said, touching his moustache which was orderly, as were his fingernails, as was the perfectly brilliantined hair plastered across his smooth skull. He was science incarnate, a sum of his own propositions, each falsifiable but never falsified. When he stared at us we saw our future. There was terror and chaos. We had to pray for order.

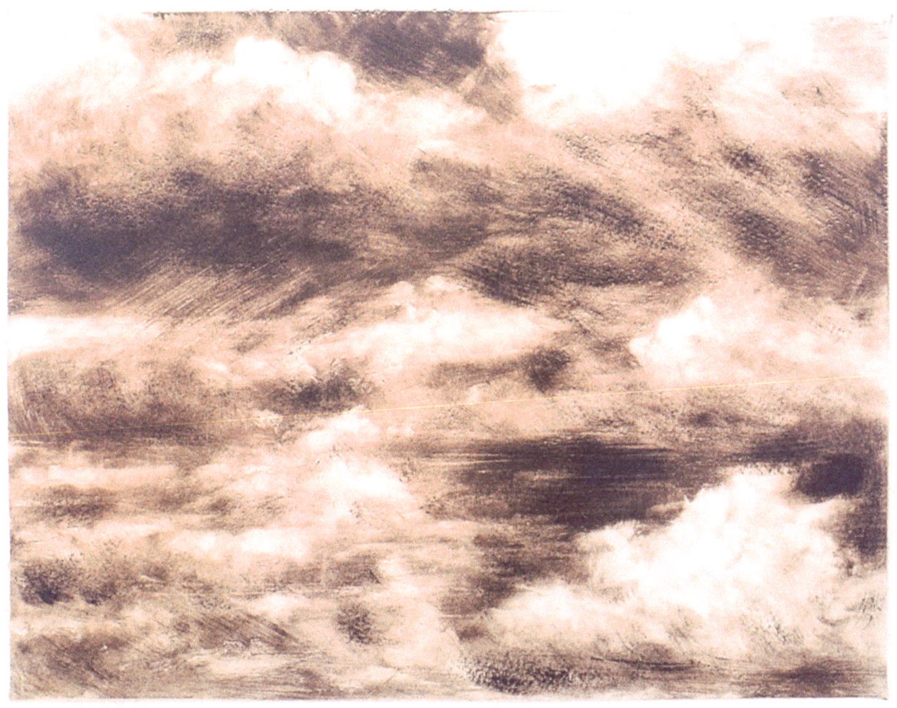

Cloud 28

Slowly
they pushed themselves
upright. They were earthbound
and heavy like Buonarotti's
breakfast.

They lay on the ground waiting for orders to rise. They were hewn from larger masses then chiselled into manageable blocks. Their inner lives had to be discovered by an official genius who would beat them with hammers time and time again. This was not what we asked for, they muttered. This must be irony, a joke of some sort. Then they grew souls and stopped joking.

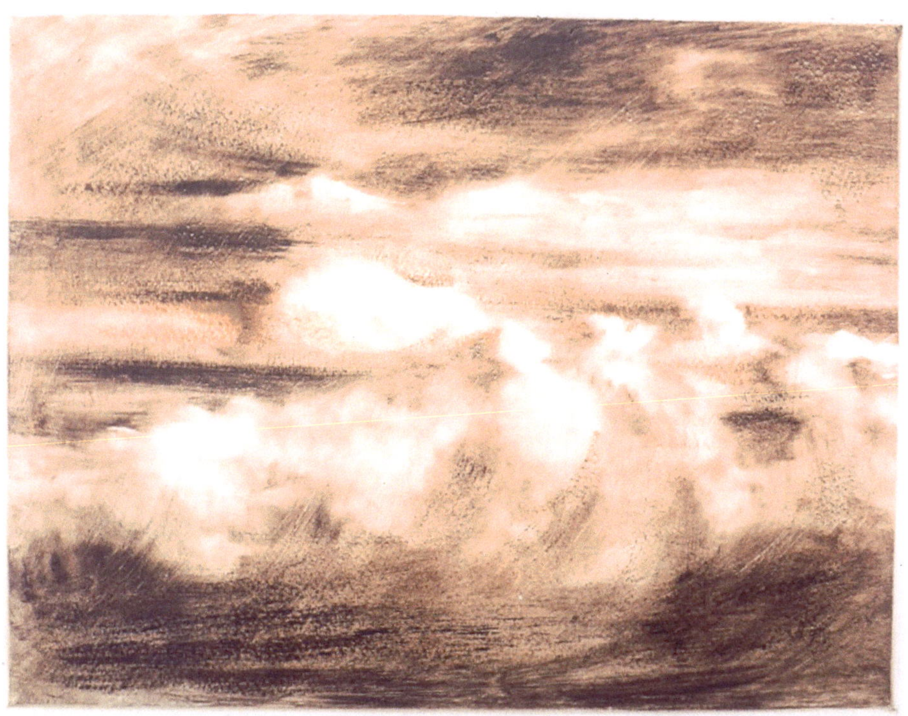

Cloud 29

Then came
a cataract
like Niagara, like
the end of a world ending in
water.

We were waiting for the president when the skies opened and centuries of rain cascaded down. He arrived with his umbrella and his folded speech. When he opened the umbrella all kinds of things fell out of it. The water was rising, up to his knee and then his thigh but he kept talking. Still the water rose. Then an army of security men came rushing with more umbrellas, the cataclysm slowly relented and there he was, a tiny president, floating.

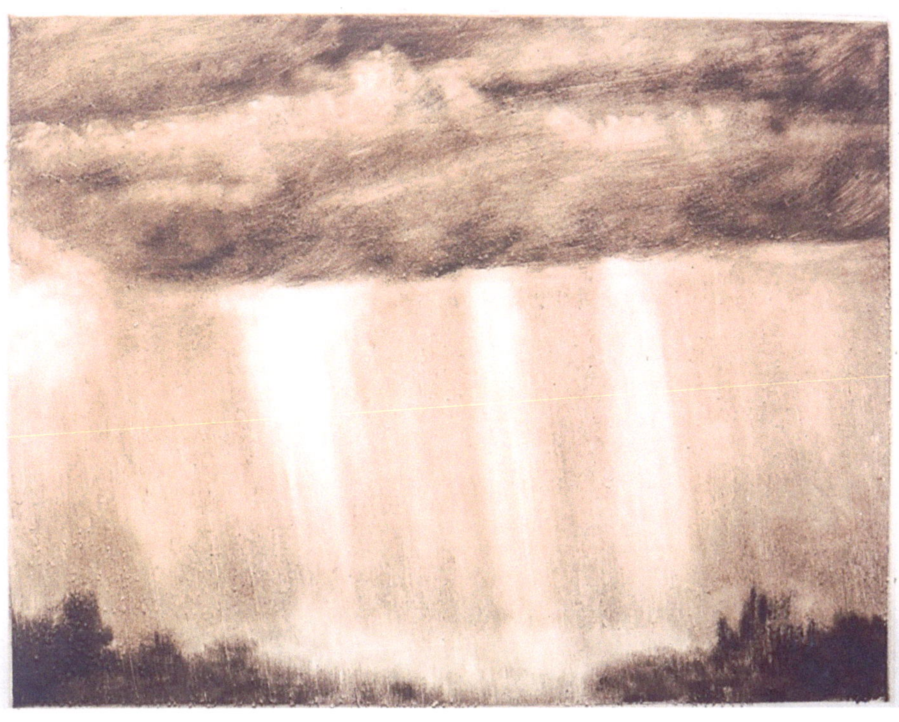

Cloud 30

The flood
had receded
and there before us stood
the mountain of ourselves, too high
to climb.

Once on a mountain road the coach slipped and we hovered in space with one wheel spinning mid-air. It was a noble sight: high peaks, the winding road, and the coach performing a miracle like a forgotten saint. No doubt there would be a shrine. No doubt there would be rain. No doubt there would be God bringing the rain down and balancing our coach on his potent finger.

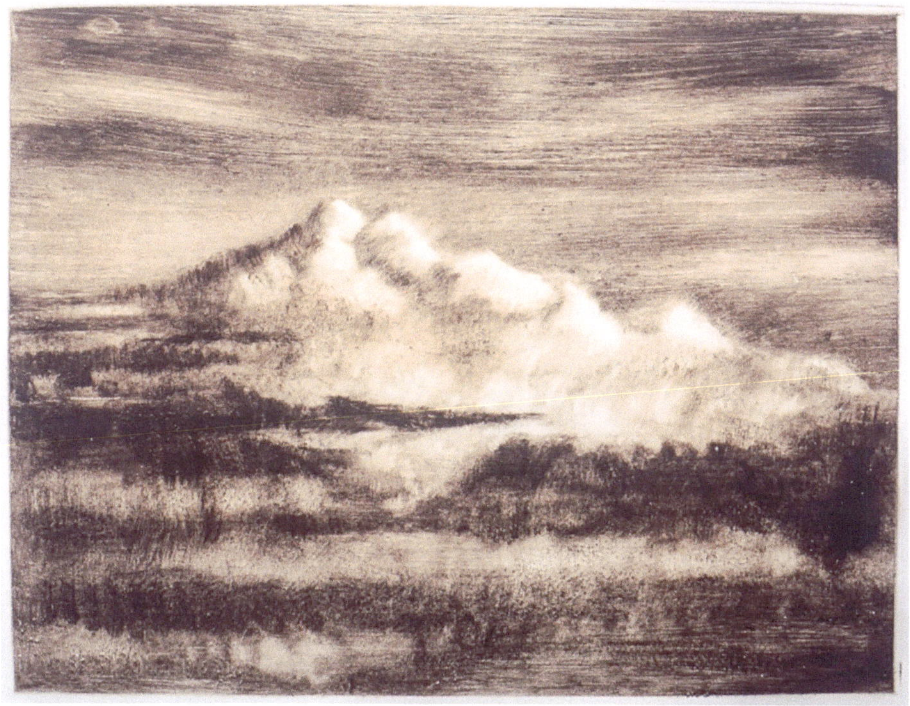

www.ingramcontent.com/pod-product-compliance
Lightning Source LLC
La Vergne TN
LVHW070219110826
845147LV00003B/607